I-SPY

with David Bellamy

ARCHAEOLOGY

I-Spy Books
12 Star Road, Partridge Green
Horsham, Sussex RH13 8RA

If you want to have your career in ruins, become an archaeologist. Real active stuff, digging up the past, and in a country like ours it's happening all the time. The results of the excavations which take tremendous knowledge, patience and skill are eventually put on display in museums, some of which are built specially for the purpose. Archaeology is where mystery stops and history starts to get exciting.

Here's your path through British pre-history, from the days when man first learnt to use flints to the time, many thousands of years later, when he had learnt how to make glass.

As you work your way through I-SPY Archaeology, refer back to this diagram; it names each period for you with a colour code, tells you how old it is and the kind of things produced then.

AD410

Glass Bottle AD43
ROMAN

AD43

Helmet, 75BC

Brooch, 250BC

IRON AGE

Pottery Bowl, 450BC

600BC

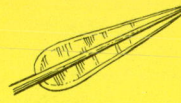

Spearhead, 1000BC

BRONZE AGE

Food Vessel, 1850BC

2400BC

Stone Axe 3000BC (Neolithic Period)

6400BC Britain separated from Continent by sea

STONE AGE

Barbed Antler Spearhead 12,000BC (Mesolithic Period)

Flint Hand Axe, 500,000BC (Palaeolithic Period)

500,000BC

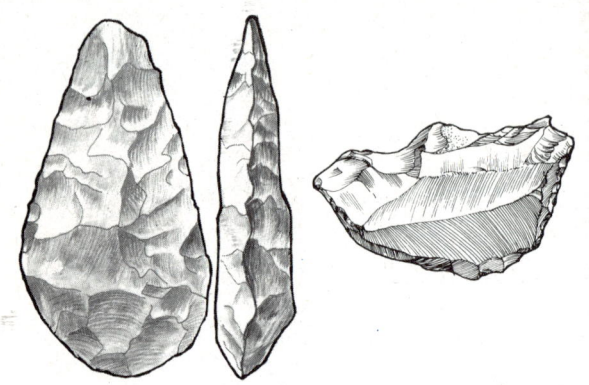

STONE AGE

His tools and weapons are in museums all over the country, but remains of Stone Age Man himself are very rare. For instance, the famous human remains found at Swanscombe, Kent, are only fragments of a skull. From these, however, archaeologists can tell that Swanscombe Man lived 250,000 years ago, belonged to the Acheulian culture (named after a site at St. Acheul, near Amiens in northern France— remember, Britain was still joined to Europe at this time!) and chipped simple tools like the flint hand axe *(top left)*.

Another culture, called Clactonian after a site discovered at Clacton, Essex, split flints into flake tools by placing them on an anvil-stone and striking them from above with another stone *(top right)*.

Score for seeing either Acheulian or Clactonian tools.

Mine was a...

at...*Museum* Score **60**

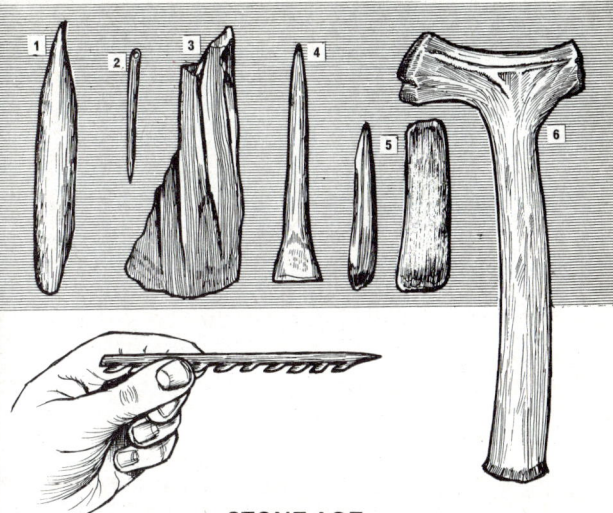

STONE AGE

By the late Stone Age men were making tools and weapons from wood, bone and antler as well as flint. Very few wooden implements have survived, but you'll see a great variety of needles, awls, wedges, chisels, hammers and harpoons made from bone and antler.

Above left, is part of a harpoon and, *top* (1) awl made of polished antler, (2) polished bone needle, (3) horse bone from which slivers have been gouged out for needles, (4) bone awl, (5) antler wedge or chisel—shown from two angles, (6) antler hammer.

Mine was a...

at.. *Museum* Score **30**

At this time there were probably only some 20,000 people in Britain. By the time the Romans invaded the population had grown to about half a million.

TANG   BARB

STONE/EARLY BRONZE AGE

Britain was cut off from the Continent about 6000BC, in the Mesolithic or Middle Stone Age. Tool-making had developed, and small flint flakes called microliths *(above left)* were being slotted into wooden or horn handles as weapons or tools. A row of very small ones made a saw. 2000 years later farming peoples began to cross the Channel, bringing pottery and domestic animals.

The leister *(below)*, a fish spear with barbed antler points, was used particularly for catching pike. Skeletons of fish 'that got away' are found with broken leister points still in them. The flint arrowhead *(above right)* was made during the Early Bronze Age and is 'barbed' and 'tanged'.

Where did you see any of these three things?........................

....Score **50**

LEISTER OR FISH SPEAR

6

f you live at the wrong end of the country to see certain types of site, you may score for spying museum exhibits of them. But you must say where you saw them.

STONE AGE/EARLY BRONZE AGE HUT CIRCLE

Traces of primitive shelters of the Mesolithic nomads are rare, but stone hut circles—remains of Neolithic (New Stone Age) and Bronze Age houses, can be seen in Cornwall, Devon and Yorkshire, and shallow depressions show where huts once stood. Most had drystone walls roofed with branches covered by turf.

Furniture was usually of wood, but at Skara Brae in Orkney shortage of timber forced the use of stone. In the hut below is a central hearth, and beyond it a bed *(left)*, and sideboard *(right)* with a small sunken tank for shellfish.

My hut circle was at .... Score **80**

SKARA BRAE

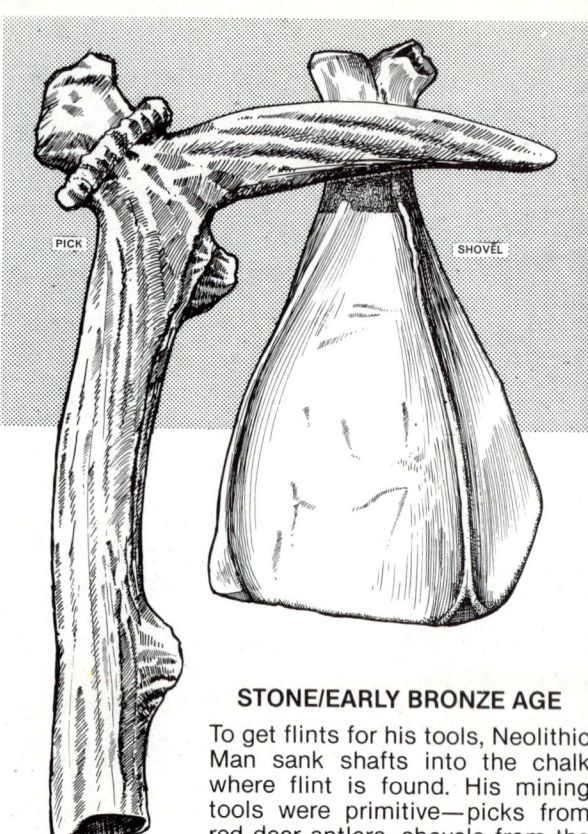

PICK

SHOVEL

STONE/EARLY BRONZE AGE

To get flints for his tools, Neolithic Man sank shafts into the chalk where flint is found. His mining tools were primitive—picks from red deer antlers, shovels from the shoulder blades of oxen—but he used them with great skill. Score for seeing any Neolithic or Bronze Age mining tool.

STONE/EARLY BRONZE AGE

Grimes Graves in Norfolk near Thetford are the best known Neolithic flint mines in Britain, with well over 300 shafts and other workings discovered. From a distance they are a confused mass of mounds and hollows, but a shaft is kept open and one can go down to look at the galleries. The name comes from later Danish settlers who thought the place must have been a burial place of their god Odin or Grimr.

(The name Grim's Dyke, given to later earthworks you may see elsewhere in England, comes from the English name Grim, given to another god, Woden.)

Mine was at...

....

....Score **90**

GRIMES GRAVES

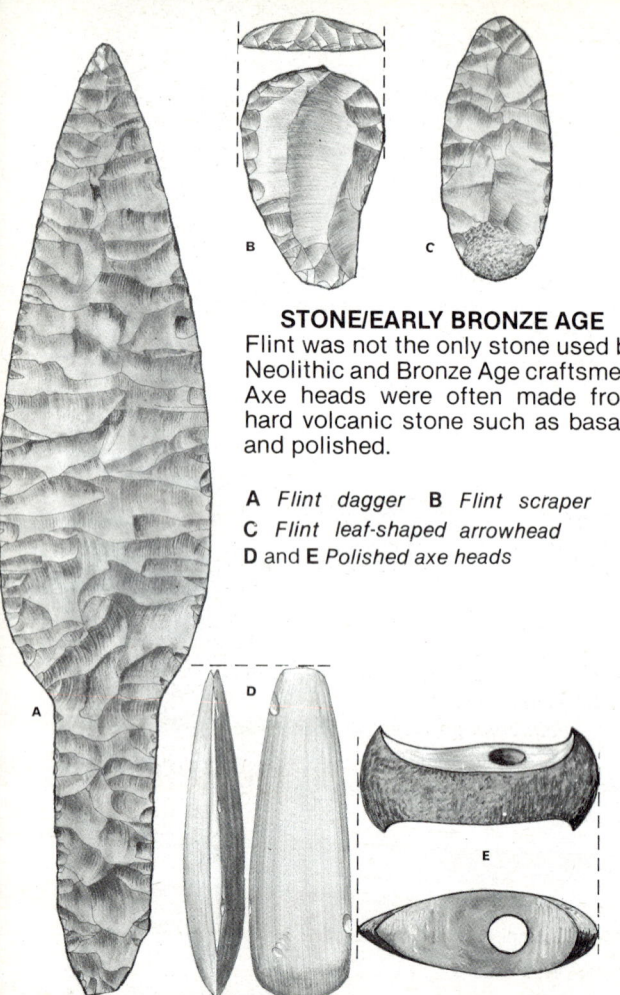

STONE/EARLY BRONZE AGE

Flint was not the only stone used by Neolithic and Bronze Age craftsmen. Axe heads were often made from hard volcanic stone such as basalt, and polished.

A *Flint dagger* **B** *Flint scraper*
C *Flint leaf-shaped arrowhead*
D and **E** *Polished axe heads*

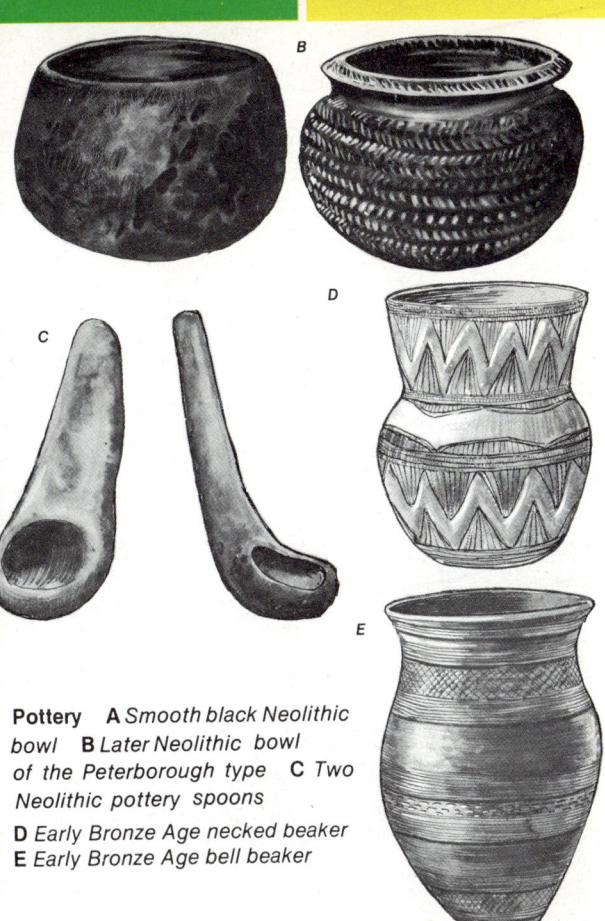

Pottery A *Smooth black Neolithic bowl* B *Later Neolithic bowl of the Peterborough type* C *Two Neolithic pottery spoons* D *Early Bronze Age necked beaker* E *Early Bronze Age bell beaker*

What have you seen similar to anything on these two pages, and where?..
....Score **40**

LONG BARROWS

Built by Neolithic farmers as a burial place for the
family of a chief or other important people, about 200
survive in England. Most are mounds of earth or chalk,
from 30.5-91 metres (100-300 feet) long, 9-31 metres
(30-100 feet) wide and 1.2-3.7 metres (4-12 feet) high.
The burial was at the higher, wider end, usually to the
east. You may see one in the middle of a field, perhaps
with a clump of trees on it.

STANDING STONES *(below)*

Found in moorland areas. Some may be natural rock,
shaped by erosion; others may be all that is left of a
megalithic tomb, a stone circle or processional way.
These three are the Devil's Arrows near Borough-
bridge, Yorkshire. 6.1 metres (20 feet) tall, they were
dragged 10.5 kilometres (6½ miles) from a quarry at
Knaresborough. They may be something to do with
stone circles and sacred sites a few miles north.

DEVIL'S ARROWS

What did you see and where?...

.... Score **70**

BRYN CELLI DDU

BRONZE AGE MEGALITHIC TOMB

Megalithic means 'made of large stones', and there are some 2000 to be found in the British Isles. They were collective burial places, for a class of people or a family group. Two main types are found. A Passage Grave has a large round mound or cairn covering a narrow passage to a central chamber. A Gallery Grave has a long stone passage, sometimes sectioned off and with side chambers, under a long mound. In many cases the mound and much of the stone has disappeared, but some are intact and may be entered. Above is Bryn Celli Ddu, a passage grave in Anglesey.

Sometimes only a capstone on supporting blocks remains. This is called a Dolmen (an old Cornish word) or, in Wales, a Cromlech. **CARREG SAMSON, DYFED**

STONEHENGE

At the time the first Stonehenge was created as a place of burial and worship, another monumental holy place was being built far away—the Great Pyramids at Giza in Egypt.

STONEHENGE

The greatest Bronze Age temple in Europe! It began as a burial place with a single stone and a circular earthwork in the Neolithic Period, about 2200 BC, and was altered several times down the centuries. Finally, about 1500BC, 80 huge stones, each weighing up to 50.8 tonnes (50 tons), were dragged 40.2 kilometres (25 miles) from the Marlborough Downs to make the great circle we see today.

What was the name of the stone circle you visited?

....Score **40**

Other stones, used earlier, came from the Prescelly Hills, 209 kilometres (130 miles) away in Wales. Archaeologists cannot decide whether they were dragged that great distance on wooden sledges, or if glaciers pushed them into the area much earlier during an Ice Age. That, and the carvings of a dagger and axe heads on some of the uprights, add to the many mysteries of Stonehenge.

Below, mortise holes in a lintel (crosspiece) fitted over knobs called tenons on the upright stones.

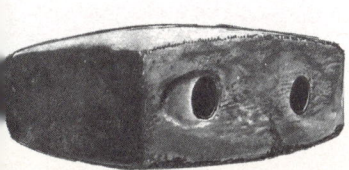

15

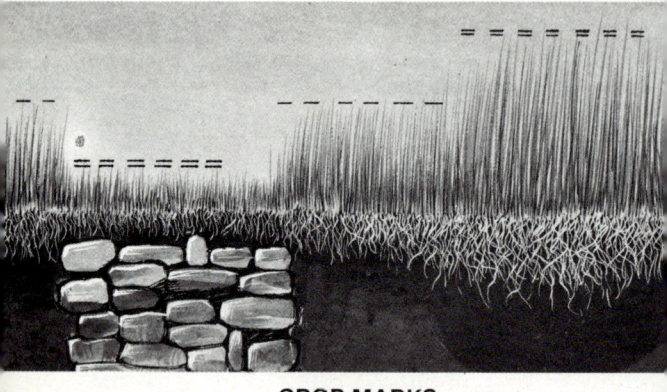

CROP MARKS

Using aircraft and cameras, archaeologists are now able to discover new sites even when there is nothing apparently visible above the ground. The reason is simple. After a hole or ditch has been dug, it gradually silts up again with soil and dead leaves. This absorbs water more easily and has a higher humus content than the land surrounding it, so vegetation grows taller on this new soil.

If, on the other hand, there is buried stonework below the surface, the shallow soil will dry out quickly and vegetation will be poor—as you can see in the diagram.

You may detect patterns in grass and other vegetation, but crops planted by man provide the best background. Barley is the most effective, followed by wheat and oats; clover is good too.

If the entire Bronze Age population of the British Isles could have gone to a Cup Final at Wembley Stadium, there'd still have been seats to spare!

When you look down from an aircraft or the top of a hill, these differences of height are transformed into patterns showing, perhaps, the outlines of buildings, trackways, forts or settlements.

So see if you can spot crop marks yourself. All you need is good luck and a hill, the steeper the better, overlooking a field of crops. The contrasts show up best after a spell of dry weather, and if the sun is shining from one side that helps too.

The crop marks in this photograph show round barrows *(see next page)*.

I-SPYed crop marks at...

....Score **100**

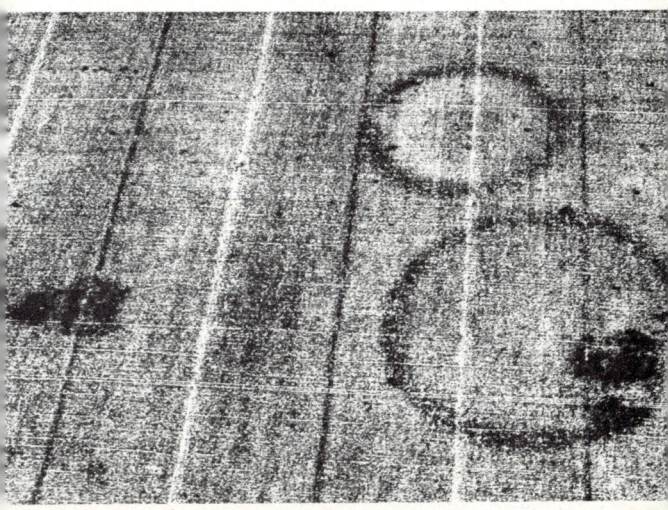

BRONZE/IRON AGE ROUND BARROWS

These are our most numerous prehistoric monuments. Despite destruction by farming and other developments, there are still between 10,000 and 20,000 round barrows in Britain (though there may once have been as many again!). They were a final covering given to the dead on a sacred spot, and may be 4.57-30.5 metres (15-100 feet) across and 6 metres (20 feet) or more high. Different types are shown below.

Bodies were often buried with tools, weapons and food to help in the next life. The tools and weapons were sometimes broken to release the spirits believed to live in them. Some are shown opposite.

Where did you see a round barrow?......................Score **40**

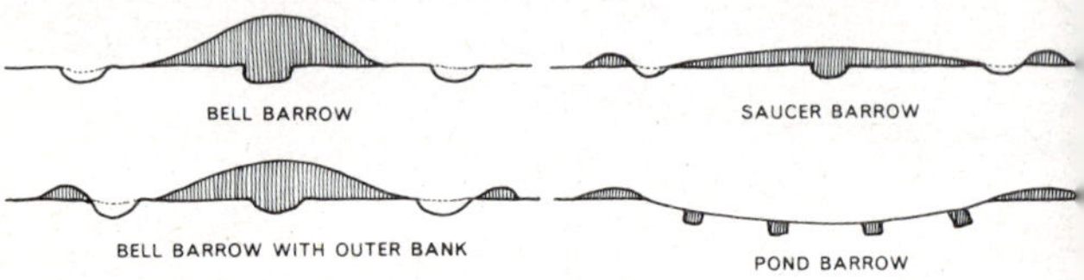

BOWL BARROW WITH DITCH

BETWEEN BELL AND DISC BARROW

BOWL WITH DITCH AND OUTER RINGS

DISC BARROW

BELL BARROW

SAUCER BARROW

BELL BARROW WITH OUTER BANK

POND BARROW

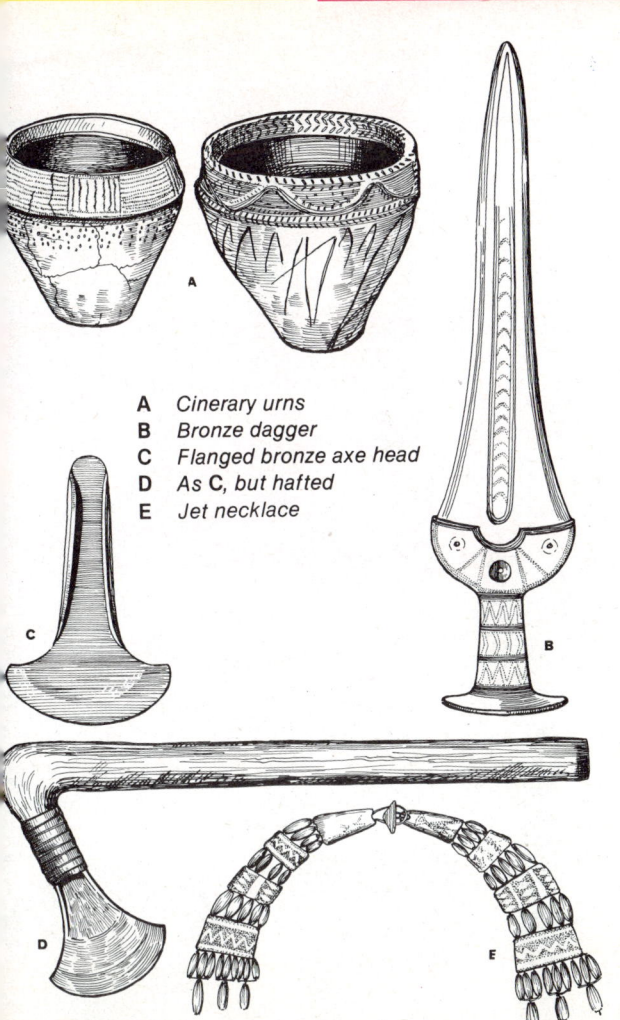

A Cinerary urns
B Bronze dagger
C Flanged bronze axe head
D As **C**, but hafted
E Jet necklace

19

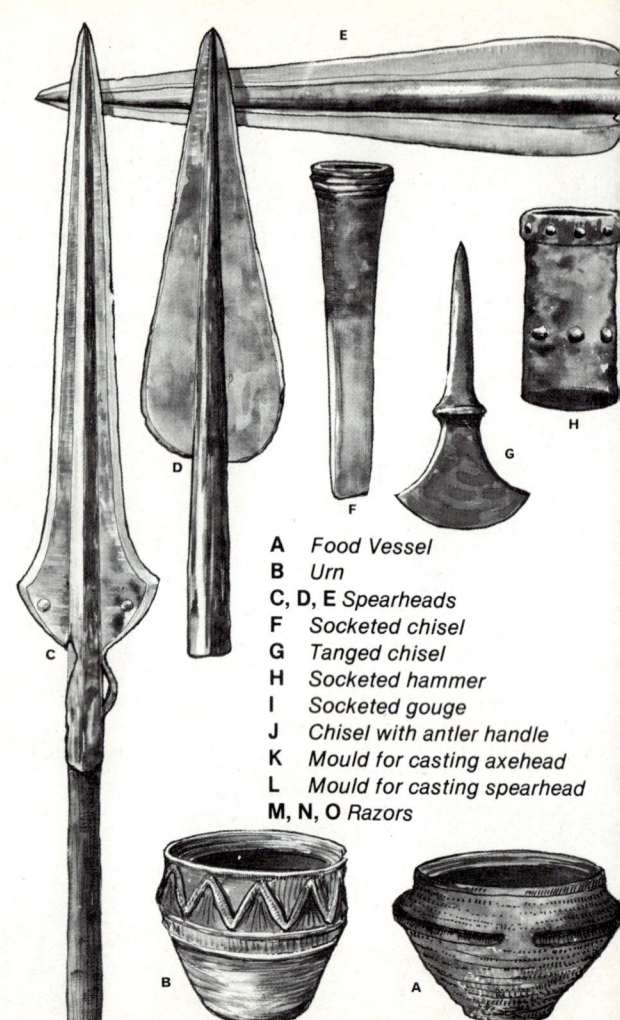

A   *Food Vessel*
B   *Urn*
C, D, E *Spearheads*
F   *Socketed chisel*
G   *Tanged chisel*
H   *Socketed hammer*
I   *Socketed gouge*
J   *Chisel with antler handle*
K   *Mould for casting axehead*
L   *Mould for casting spearhead*
M, N, O *Razors*

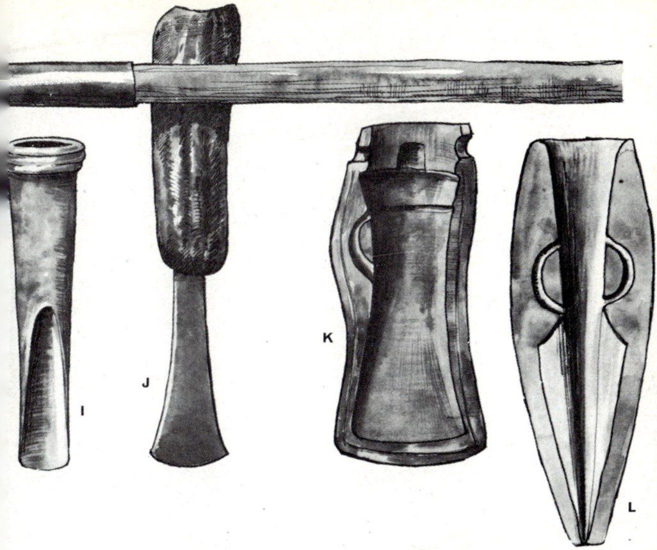

I

J

K

L

From about 2400 BC Britain was settled by the Beaker peoples (so named from their distinctive pottery) from areas of present day Germany, Denmark and Holland. They brought knowledge of metalworking, first in copper and later in bronze.

Name three Bronze Age articles you have seen..................
....Score **30**

O

N

M

Bronze is an alloy of copper with a small amount of tin, and was discovered when copper ore that was being melted contained traces also of tin, that became fused. Bronze is stronger than copper and does not rust, and is used to this day for outdoor statues.

BRONZE AGE CELTIC FIELDS

An improved plough, called the Ard, was developed during the Middle Bronze Age. Pulled by oxen, it was worked along and then across the plot, to break up the soil thoroughly. The small Celtic fields, as they are called, were square or oblong for convenience, and traces are still to be seen on open land. Here are some at Chilcombe Down, Dorset.

This system continued through the Iron Age and into the Roman Period.

Mine were at...Score **60**

CHILCOMBE DOWN

IRON AGE

Settlers continued to cross the Channel bringing new ideas, and by 600 BC iron-working had arrived. Iron ore was commoner than copper and tin, and didn't need alloying, so more people had more tools for all sorts of work. Carpenters' and farmers' tools became very like those still used today.

Note the increasing interest in ornament.

What is the most interesting Iron Age tool you have seen?...Score **40**

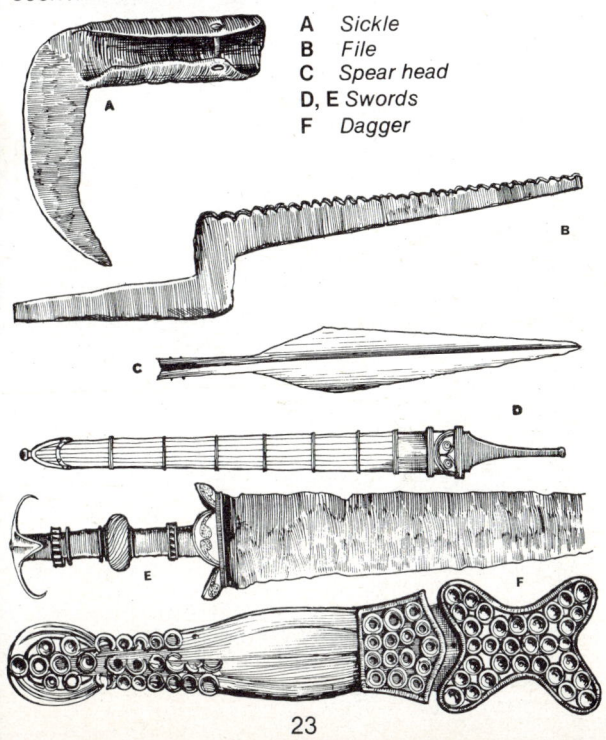

A   *Sickle*
B   *File*
C   *Spear head*
D, E *Swords*
F   *Dagger*

IRON AGE

Chieftains of the Iron Age Celtic tribes were sometimes buried with their war chariots. Look in museums for their helmets, shields, horse-harness and chariot fittings.

Here are:
A *Horned helmet from the Thames by Waterloo Bridge*
B *Helmet with a broad neck guard probably from northern Britain*

C *Bronze bridle bit from a Yorkshire chariot burial*
D *Hollow bronze horn from County Limerick*
E *Gold-bronze shield from the Thames at Battersea*

BRONZE SCABBARD WITH CHASED SCROLL-ORNAMENT

IRON AGE

Marvellous styles of decorative art came in from the Continent, first through the Parisi tribe settling East Yorkshire in the 3rd century BC. Glass was unknown, so mirrors were made of highly polished bronze and their backs, like many other objects, were highly decorated. This one was found at Desborough, Northants, and there is a similar one from Birdlip in Gloucestershire.

What were the Iron Age articles you saw and where did you see them?..
....Score **30**

E

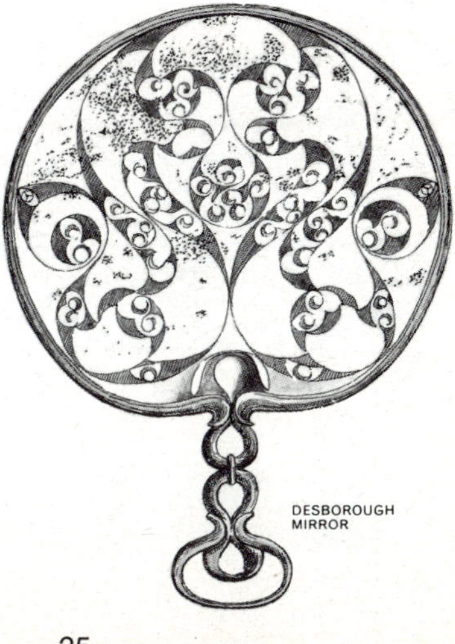

DESBOROUGH
MIRROR

25

IRON AGE

Farming tribes in the early Iron Age protected themselves with hilltop forts—an outer ditch and a revetment (a wall of stone or wooden stakes) with earth ramparts behind. Between the ditch and the revetment was a berm, an exposed shelf on which attackers would come under a hail of missiles from the defenders.

Here's another form of defence, a Scottish broch; a tall circular tower built as a stronghold by an Iron Age chief who probably combined farming with raiding.

Where was your Iron Age hill fort?...
....Score **60**

As weapons improved and new ones such as the sling were introduced, the strength of hill forts had to increase. It may have worked the other way too—new weapons being needed to overcome stronger defences. Later hill forts had extra ramparts and entrances devised so that attackers couldn't storm straight in.

MAIDEN CASTLE

The famous Maiden Castle in Dorset *(above)* was once a Neolithic causewayed camp (causeways across surrounding ditches and gaps in ramparts). It then became an early Iron Age fort and finally one of the most important forts in Britain. It fell to the Roman Second Legion in AD 44.

The many fascinating finds included large piles of sling stones by the gateways for use by the defenders.

The Parisi people, who made their capital in England at Brough, came from the Seine and Marne area of France and took their name from their chief town there—Paris. So Yorkshire Spyers could be related to present day Parisians!

IRON AGE

A small group of late Iron Age people built villages on artificial islands in marshes at Glastonbury and Meare in Somerset. They were abandoned when the Romans came, and were gradually overlaid by moist marsh peat. This has preserved much that seldom survives on a hill village site—carts, dug-out canoes, baskets, wooden bowls, knives still with their hafts—and tells us a great deal about everyday life in the late Iron Age.

Model of Glastonbury lake-village huts

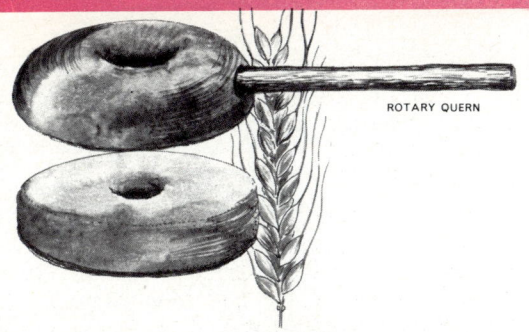

ROTARY QUERN

IRON AGE

The people of the lake villages used the new rotary stone quern with a wooden handle for grinding their corn, and their pottery can be recognized by its graceful wavy decoration. The potter's wheel was introduced in this period, and pottery became a specialized craft.

Look at the pottery for horizontal streak marks left by the potter's fingers 2000 years ago! You may also see marks on the base, showing how the pot was detached from the wheel by sawing across with a length of string held in both hands. Spy both these marks (shown below) on later Iron Age pots, and note where you saw them.

Finger marks...Score **40**

String marks...Score **40**

Stater (left, top and bottom) and Celtic copies.

IRON AGE

As well as bringing the rotary quern and potter's wheel, the Belgae (tribes from present day Belgium) introduced wheeled vehicles and coinage. Until then trade had been by barter, or with flat iron currency bars serving as money. Their first coins were copied from those of Roman-occupied Gaul (France), and from the gold stater of Philip of Macedon (Greece). In the process of copying, the original design gradually altered until completely unrecognizable *(above)*.

Where did you see your Iron Age currency?........................

....Score **80**

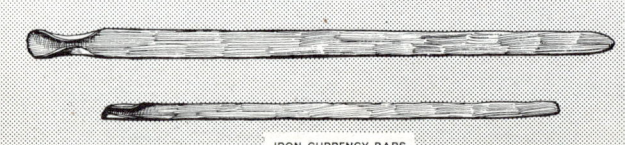

IRON CURRENCY BARS

IRON AGE

The long, lean figure of a horse—a Celtic version of a Greek design, appears on many Iron Age coins, and one is to be seen cut into a chalk hillside at Uffington, Berkshire. Some say it was cut by King Alfred after his victory at Ashdown against the Danes in 871, or that it was to represent the dragon slain by St. George. But it was probably cut in the 1st century BC by the tribe who held Uffington Castle hill fort close by.

Not all hill figures date from the Iron Age. Most are medieval or quite recent. Two others that are probably Celtic are the Cerne Abbas Giant, Dorset, and the Long Man of Wilmington, Sussex.

Which early hill figure have you seen? ....

....Score **50**

White Horse at Uffington, Berkshire

ROMAN

Julius Caesar made landings in Kent in 55 and 54 BC, and fought the Celtic war chariots as far north as Hertfordshire. A century later, in AD 43, the Emperor Claudius ordered the full invasion.

A bridge across the Thames was built, and docks and the city of Londinium followed. Later the Celts were to call it London, and that first bridge was just 55 metres (60 yards) downstream from the present London Bridge.

In AD 60 the Iceni tribe from Norfolk, led by their Queen Boudica (Boadicea), stormed Londinium and destroyed it by fire. It was gradually rebuilt to become the capital of the province of Britain. By the end of the second century a wall 3.2 kilometres (2 miles) long was built round the city *(see inside front cover)*. Sections like the one below still remain.

Opposite are some of the other fortifications to be seen in Britain:

A *Newport Arch, Lincoln*   **B** *Burgh Castle, Great Yarmouth;* **C** *Multangular Tower, York*   **D** *Bastion and town wall, Caerwent.*

I saw Roman fortifications at

.... Score **50**

CITY WALL, LONDON

LINCOLN

BURGH CASTLE

YORK

CAERWENT

In the summer of the AD43 invasion, the Emperor Claudius came over to inspect things, and brought a troop of elephants to impress the locals!

ROMAN

Their roads are one of the most lasting impressions we have of the Romans. They were built to link towns and forts, to be used all the year round in all weathers, and we travel on many of them today. Some of our most historic towns are linked by them.

They were often built along an aggar, or embankment, with a ditch on either side, and where possible ran for great distances in a straight line. This air photograph is of the Fosse Way, which ran from Lincoln to Exeter. We have built our modern road exactly on top of the Roman one.

Stone foundation layers of some Roman roads are still to be seen, as are milestones. Score for walking or driving along any Roman road—whether a modern highway, a narrow lane between high hedges or just a faint ridge across a field.

Mine was at..Score **30**

34

ROMAN

Much of England was conquered, but warring tribes and difficult country gave the Romans problems in Wales and Scotland. They built great fortresses at Caerleon (in Gwent), Chester and York, each covering 20.2 hectares (50 acres) and holding a Legion of 6000 men. The Emperor Hadrian came over to supervise construction of a wall right the way across the north of England, from the mouth of the Tyne to the Solway Firth. It was 117.5 kilometres (73 miles) long, up to 6 metres (20 feet) high and mostly built of stone. At every mile point was a small fort or milecastle and between each were two observation turrets. All along the north side was a huge ditch, 2.7 metres (9 feet) deep and 8.2 metres (27 feet) wide. Much of this great feat of engineering remains.

Hadrian's Wall is famous. Less well known is the Antonine Wall, further north, ordered by Hadrian's successor Antoninus Pius. It ran for 59.5 kilometres (37 miles), from the Forth to the Clyde, and was built of turf with an even bigger ditch, 3.7 metres (12 feet) deep and 12.2 metres (40 feet) wide. Traces remain, particularly of the ditch and of forts.

Which Roman fort have you seen? ....

.... Score **50**

HADRIAN'S WALL

ROMAN

Many towns date from the Roman period. Some began as trading settlements outside forts. Others, such as Gloucester, were developed for soldiers demobilised from the legions. Lincoln is another *colonia* of this kind.

Outside the walls of many towns were amphitheatres for public games, spectacles and gladiator fights.

An important part of Roman social life were the public baths—more like saunas than swimming baths, with cold, warm and hot rooms. A metal strigil was used to scrape off sweat and grime, and olive oil rubbed in to soften the skin again.

Opposite:

A *oil flask and strigils* **B** *nail cleaner with tweezers* **C** *bone comb* **D** *ligula, for taking cosmetics from the narrow glass phials they were kept in* **E** *ear scoop*

Score for seeing any Roman amphitheatre, bath or hypocaust—an underfloor heating system shown below.
What did you see, where?..
....Score **60**

Hypocaust at Chedworth Roman Villa, Glos. A floor once covered the pillars, and hot air circulated to heat the room above.

ROMAN
BATHS,
BATH

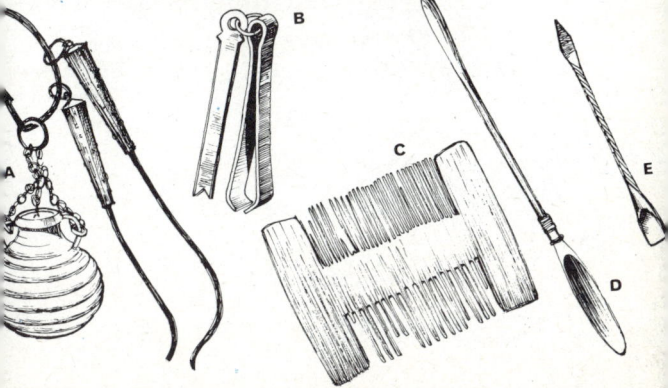

A

B

C

D

E

In a pile of Roman rubbish excavated on the site of the Central Criminal Court, Old Bailey, were found the clay moulds of a Roman coin forger!

ROMAN TOOLS

A *saw* **B** *combined axe and hammer* **C** *carpenter's chisel*
D *two drill bits for fitting into a brace*

AMPHORA

Wine and olive oil was shipped from Italy, Spain and Gaul in large pottery jars called amphorae. When of this shape they were stacked on their sides or stood in holes in the ground.

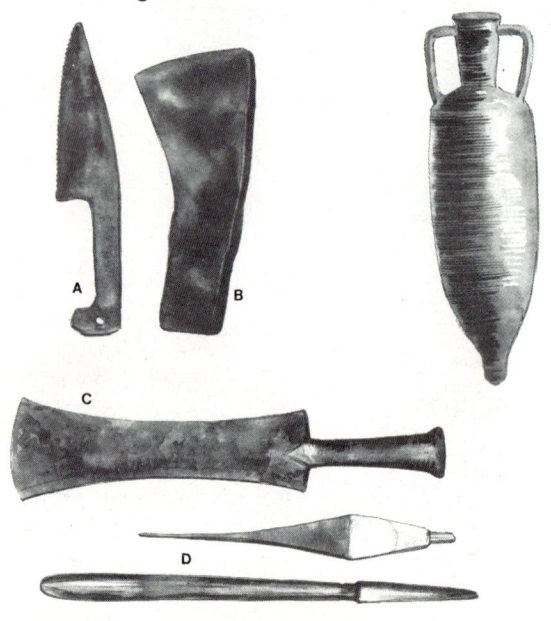

RELIGION

After prohibiting the Druids—a Celtic priesthood, the Romans were very tolerant about which gods the Britons worshipped. They even added Celtic gods to their own long list of deities. *Below left,* an altar, one of a group a centurion dedicated to twelve different gods.

CHI-RHO MONOGRAM

Christianity became the official religion in AD 312. Chi and Rho are the first two letters of the word 'Christ' in Greek, and in the form of a monogram *below right,* are often to be seen on villa walls and floors and on pewter and silverware.

Score for anything on these two pages.

What did you see, where?...

....Score **40**

39

LULLINGSTONE VILLA

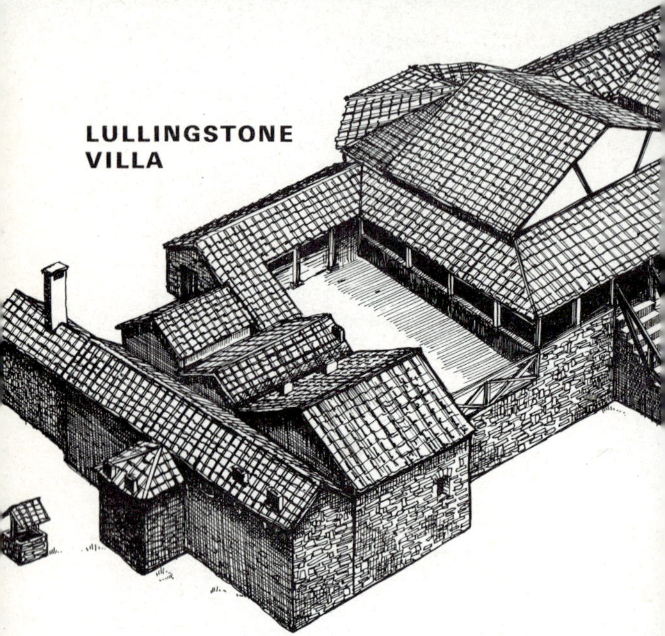

CUP

BOWL

ROMAN

Wealthy Romans often built luxurious villas on their estates. Here is a reconstruction of Lullingstone villa in Kent. Built near the end of the first century it stood for 300 years, a succession of owners making various alterations until it was destroyed by fire.

Twelve years of careful excavation have given us much to see, including beautiful mosaics. One is on the front cover; another still bears the marks of burning rafters that fell on it.

The fine hard, red imported pottery is called Samian ware. Pottery was also made locally for everyday use. Below left, Samian cup and bowl.

Glassware (below) and window glass were imported in great quantities. Only four glass furnaces have been found in Britain: at Wroxeter, Salop; Mancetter, Warwicks; Wilderspool, Cheshire; and Caister near Norwich, where the Romans built a tribal capital for the defeated Iceni (page 32).

I saw a villa at...Score **80**

Look for the typical colours and iridescence in Roman glass.

GLASS FLASKS AND BOTTLES
(all bluish green in colour)

If you ever find anything of interest, take it to your local museum and they will identify it. If it is of value it might be declared to be Treasure Trove, in which case you will be paid its full worth and it will go into the museum's collection, with your name on the label!

ROMAN KITCHEN

Reconstruction of a Roman kitchen, at the Museum of London. I-SPY the amphorae and mosaic.

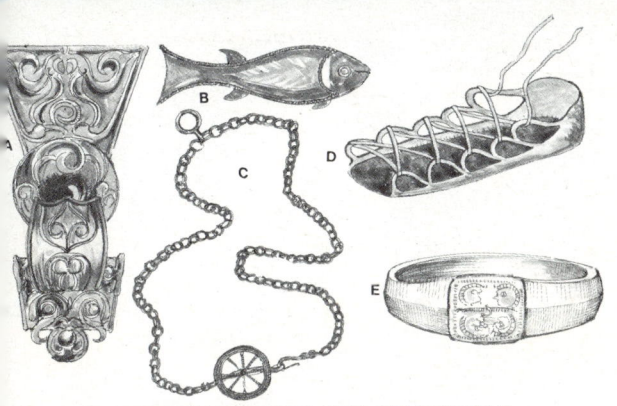

ROMAN ORNAMENTS AND FOOTWEAR

A   Celtic-style brooch, decorated in true Celtic manner with embossed scrolls. A good example of the way native art continued to flourish during Roman occupation.

B   Roman brooch, used instead of a button. Bronze, with green and white enamel (vitreous enamel, made of glass-like coloured powders fused on to the metal by melting in a kiln).

C   Gold chain, a personal ornament.

D   Sandal. A man's sandal that laced up round the lower leg. Boots with studded soles, sandals and leather scraps are sometimes found in areas where Roman shoemakers had shops—near the Bank of England in London, for instance.

E   Finger ring. Silver, engraved with four helmeted heads.

What Roman ornament have you seen?..............................

....Score **40**

43

ROMAN WRITING

Romans wrote by scratching on wax-surfaced wooden tablets with sharply pointed metal styli, and with ink on parchment with split-nibbed pens rather like those we use today.

Inkwells *(above)* The one on the left is of pottery; the smaller one is of bronze, with a lid, and had loopholes for carrying it strung on a cord.

Pen *(left)* Split-nibbed pen of bronze.

Seal box *(left)* This protected the wax seal on string that was tied round a letter or document.

What writing object have you seen?..

....Score **40**

Wooden writing tablet *(below)* to be coated with wax.

ROMAN BURIAL

The Romans were forbidden to bury their dead within towns so cemeteries and tombs are usually found along the roads outside.

CINERARY URN

After cremation, ashes were buried in stone, pottery or glass urns. The lead canister below contained a glass cinerary urn.

TOMB

Usually dedicated to the gods of the underworld. Look for the words Dis Manibus (To the Spirits of the Dead), sometimes abbreviated to D.M. *Below* is the reconstructed tomb of Julius Classicianus, procurator (civil governor) of Britain.

What burial object have you seen?...
....Score **40**

CANISTER

CINERARY URN

What a fantastic heritage, there for us to see, experience and enjoy; and, what is more, in a country like ours, so much more still waiting to be discovered.

However, A WORD OF WARNING: DO NOT GO IT ALONE. *Don't* become one of those greedy treasure hunters who rush around the countryside with a metal detector. They rarely find anything of value and while they go their own selfish way they can cause great damage and often destroy important parts of our historical heritage.

A buried artifact can only tell its full story if it is studied where it lies and in relation to all the soil strata both above and below it. Those strata are the pages of the history book, the artifacts are mere illustrations which only have real relevance as part of the text. If you'd like to get involved in archaeology, go along and have a word with your local museum. They may well be able to tell you about local excavations, or 'digs' where untrained helpers are welcome, and will tell you about courses you can attend that include site visits.

DIG FOR HISTORY UNDER SUPERVISION. DIGGING FOR SELF GAIN IS VANDALISM OF THE WORST SORT.

JOIN THE I-SPY CLUB

- All you need to join the I-SPY Club is to buy a Membership Book which includes the secret codes. Ask at your bookshop or newsagent.

- Tell your friends about I-SPY. Invite them to join and form a Patrol with you.

- Collect all the I-SPY books—and you'll have a wonderful library of your own.

- Write to me about any interesting discoveries you make. You may win a prize! Remember to enclose a stamped addressed envelope for a reply.

LOOK OUT FOR THESE I-SPY WITH DAVID BELLAMY BOOKS

AT THE AIRPORT	CIVIL AIRCRAFT
ARCHAEOLOGY	DINOSAURS
AT THE ART GALLERY	FISH AND FISHING
BIRDS AND REPTILES AT THE ZOO	FRUITS AND FUNGI
	GARDEN FLOWERS
BRITISH COINS	ALL THE YEAR ROUND
BRITISH WILDLIFE	GARDEN BIRDS
CREEPY CRAWLIES	MAMMALS AT THE ZOO
ON A CAR JOURNEY	ON A TRAIN JOURNEY
CAR NUMBERS	TREES
CARS	WILD FLOWERS

AND MANY **MORE!** TO COME

INDEX

ACKNOWLEDGEMENTS

I-SPY thank the following for photographs: Aerofilms, Anthony Howarth, British Tourist Authority, J Allan Cash Ltd, Janet & Colin Bord, Peter Clayton, Susan Griggs Agency, The Museum of London, Unichrome and 'Shell Times' for David Bellamy's photograph on page 2. Series Editor Anthony Maynard.

Published by Ravette Limited, 12 Star Road, Partridge Green, Horsham, West Sussex RH13 8RA © Ravette Ltd. 1983. Printed in Italy (KEL) ISBN 0-906710-25-I